W9-AUY-640

Editor: PENNY CLARKE

Produced by
THE SALARIYA BOOK CO. LTD
25 Marlborough Place
Brighton BN1 5UB
England

Published by
PETER BEDRICK BOOKS
156 Fifth Avenue
New York, NY 10010

Published by agreement with
Macdonald Young Books Ltd, England

Library of Congress Cataloging-in-Publication
Data

Morley, Jacqueline.
    First facts about the Vikings / written by Jacqueline
Morley : illustrated by Mark Bergin : created and designed by
David Salariya.
        p.   cm.
    Includes index.
    Summary: Provides facts about those hardy Scandinavians
who flourished from 800 to 1100.
    ISBN 0-87226-497-1
    1. Vikings--Juvenile literature.   [I. Vikings.]
I. Bergin, Mark, ill.   II. Salariya, David.   III. Title.
DL65.M779   1996
948.022--dc20   96-12301
                                     CIP
                                     AC

Second Printing, 1998
Printed in Hong Kong.

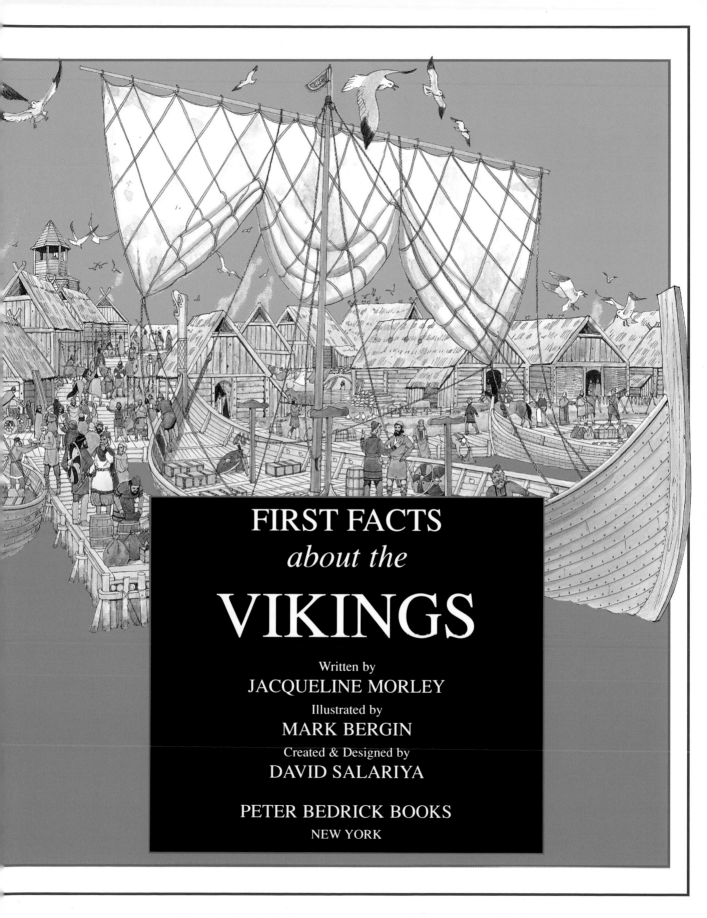

FIRST FACTS
about the
VIKINGS

Written by
JACQUELINE MORLEY

Illustrated by
MARK BERGIN

Created & Designed by
DAVID SALARIYA

PETER BEDRICK BOOKS

NEW YORK

Contents

Introduction

VIKINGS spent all their time raiding, and looting and they killed anyone who got in their way, right? That's the idea most people have of them, but is it true? Why did so many of them leave their homes to cross rough seas in small boats? Their ancestors had lived for centuries in the lands we call Scandinavia: Norway, Sweden and Denmark. They were farmers, fishermen and traders. By the 8th century they were moving into other lands around the Baltic Sea. But the rest of Europe ignored the Vikings until the 9th century, when boatloads of raiders began to attack the coasts of Britain, Ireland, France, Spain and the Mediterranean. They settled in Iceland and Greenland. A few even reached America.

For 300 years, from about 790 to 1100 the Vikings raided, traded and explored further than any Europeans before them. It took courage, or desperation, to sail out of sight of land across the Atlantic – no other sailors would attempt this until Christopher Columbus in 1492.

THERE are Viking remains in Newfoundland, proving Viking tales of finding a land in the far west are true.

FACT: MOST VIKINGS WERE QUIET HOME-LOVERS

THE VIKINGS were farmers and traders. Those who could earn a reasonable living were usually content to stay where they were. Some lived in quite large towns. These were good meeting places where people brought things to buy and sell. Below is the town of Hedeby in the land of the Danish Vikings. Like all Viking towns it was built near water. That was essential. Water was the easiest way to travel or to transport goods. Carts were slow and could not cross rough, boggy land or mountains.

Facts about Viking Homes:

Hedeby covered about 60 acres. This was big for a Viking town. Birka in Sweden was about half this size.

Most houses measured 20 by 50 feet and lasted about 30 years. When too rotten to repair, they were pulled down and rebuilt.

There were no windows, just a hole at the top of each end wall.

Cleaning the house was not very important. Rubbish on the floor was swept out every so often.

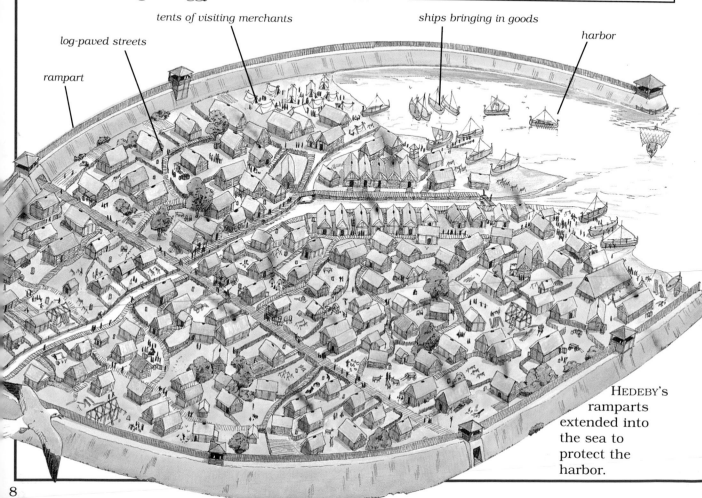

tents of visiting merchants

ships bringing in goods

harbor

log-paved streets

rampart

HEDEBY's ramparts extended into the sea to protect the harbor.

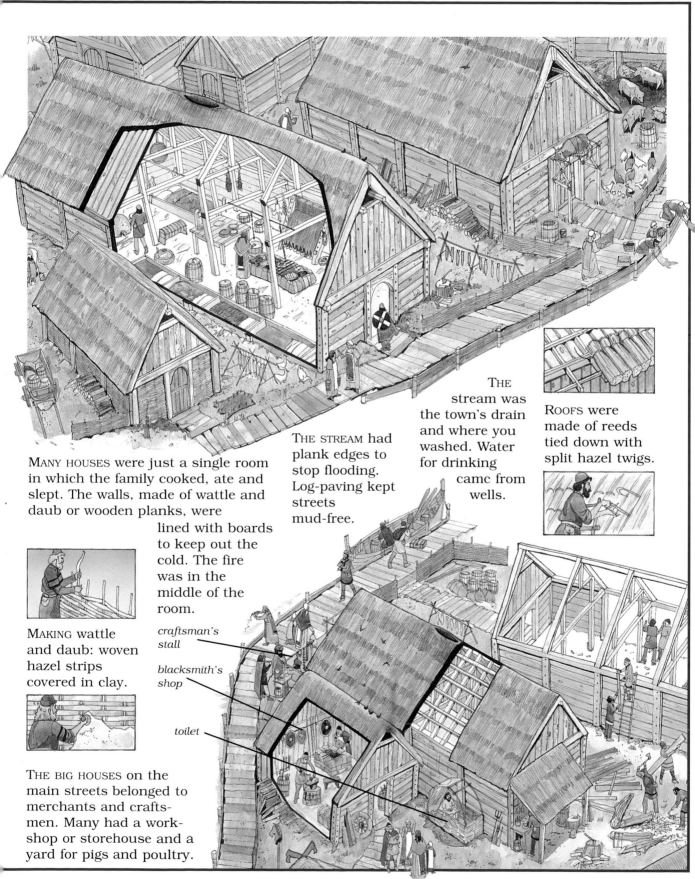

MANY HOUSES were just a single room in which the family cooked, ate and slept. The walls, made of wattle and daub or wooden planks, were lined with boards to keep out the cold. The fire was in the middle of the room.

MAKING wattle and daub: woven hazel strips covered in clay.

THE BIG HOUSES on the main streets belonged to merchants and crafts-men. Many had a work-shop or storehouse and a yard for pigs and poultry.

THE STREAM had plank edges to stop flooding. Log-paving kept streets mud-free.

THE stream was the town's drain and where you washed. Water for drinking came from wells.

ROOFS were made of reeds tied down with split hazel twigs.

craftsman's stall

blacksmith's shop

toilet

FACT: A VIKING'S FAMILY WAS LOYAL

OFTEN three generations lived together. Everyone helped in running the home and the family farm or workshop.

FOOD was kept in jars or barrels. The woman above is packing down salted meat.

A VIKING home was the family workplace. There was little room for furniture, just a few stools and perhaps a bed for the head-man and his wife. Most people slept on quilts on a low platform along the wall.

WHEN comrades vowed brother-hood it was a binding promise of loyalty.

A VIKING was always loyal. Anyone who was not was despised. People sided with their own relations, even if they had done wrong. A Viking family was a wide network, with uncles, aunts and cousins usually living close to each other. They all helped each other. If any member was attacked or insulted, all the others were ready to take revenge. Families had extra protection if the men were followers of jarls. Jarls were powerful local chieftains, with lots of land. Less wealthy freemen were farmers or traders. They had the right to carry weapons and if they owned land they could take part in local decision making. The poorest freemen might be servants. Below them were the thralls. They were slaves and had no rights at all.

Facts about Viking Families:
In winter in the far north there are weeks with little daylight and temperatures below zero, so Viking life was hard.

To marry, a couple drank 'bridal ale' before witnesses. The man paid a 'brideprice' for his wife. She had a dowry from her father, which was repaid on divorce.

Some unusual grounds for divorce were, for instance, a wife who wore pants or a husband whose shirt was too fancy for a man.

VIKINGS liked children to show spirit. No one admired weaklings. Boys and girls had to work hard, and boys were trained to fight. In the Viking world, strong people did best.

THERE were no schools. Skills were taught at home.

MARRIAGES were arranged, but divorce was easy. The husband or wife had only to tell witnesses that the marriage was over and say why.

CHILDREN learned by helping their parents. Listening to tales of brave ancestors was part of learning. It developed family pride.

THRALLS were people captured in raids or their descendants.

QUARRELS could start blood feuds between families. If the victim's family took revenge, there would be tit-for-tat killings and house burnings.

VIKINGS despised cowards. No Viking would desert a leader he had promised to support. He must fight to the death. Then his widow and children could be proud of him.

FACT: VIKINGS' LIFE WAS HARSH

gutting fish

MOST VIKINGS lived in cold lands with hard winters. Even in good years farmers struggled to produce enough food for everyone. A wet summer could mean starvation. If there was no grain there was no bread; if there was no hay cattle could not survive the winter. This gave Vikings a tough view of life. The old and the ill were not fed when food was short. Children were usually well cared for because they were the workers of the future, but if a new baby was sickly it was left to die. No family could risk having to feed a useless person for a lifetime.

Cooking was done by the women of the family. If there were no servants, children helped as soon as they could.

Facts about the Vikings' Diet:

A rich Viking's diet: as much red meat as possible, chicken, fish, eggs, cheese, wheat bread, ale or imported Frankish wine.

Diet of a poor Viking: meat broth, wild leeks, porridge and barley bread, with ale to drink.

COOKING was done on a raised hearth. Food was spit-roasted, baked over the fire or stewed in a cauldron hung from the ceiling.

FOOD was eaten from wooden platters.

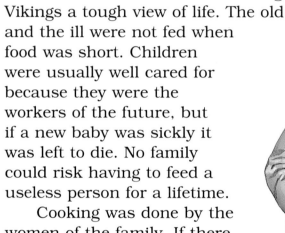

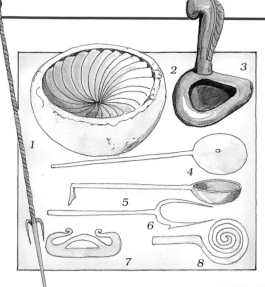

COOKING UTENSILS:
1 Roasting spear
2 Bowl
3 Wooden ladle
4 Iron spatula
5 Iron ladle
6 Skewering fork
7 Spark-striker
8 Toasting iron.

WHEN there was plenty of fresh meat and fish it was preserved for later. Fish was dried and smoked and meat was salted.

IN MAY AND JUNE seabirds nested on the cliffs. This was the time to gather eggs.

VIKINGS ate as much protein as they could: whale meat, beef, mutton, pork, reindeer, fish and seal.

TO MAKE BREAD grain was ground to flour in a quern. The flour was mixed with yeast and water and left to rise. Then it was baked.

BELOW: A farming family's evening meal: fish, ham, leeks and bread.

DRINKING HORNS were emptied in one gulp, so it did not matter that they did not stand upright.

IN SUMMER there were wild fruit and berries to eat. In autumn there were nuts and mushrooms.

VIKINGS used knives and their fingers.

FACT: VIKINGS WERE SKILLED AT MAKING THINGS

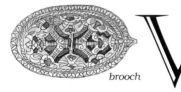

brooch

VIKINGS needed to know how to make things. Families on isolated farms had to be self-sufficient. The men had to be carpenters and blacksmiths as well as farmers. They felled timber, put up buildings, made wagons, sledges, furniture and plows. They forged tools and weapons from iron and made leather from animals' hides for harnesses, boots and capes. The women made butter, cheese and ale. They also made all the cloth the family needed. After sheepshearing they carded the wool. Then, in every spare minute, they spun it into the thread from which they would weave cloth for clothes, blankets and wall hangings. People living near towns did not have to make all these things because they could buy them in markets – but of course they were still hand-made.

VIKING men wore cloaks pinned on the left shoulder to leave the sword arm free.

tunic

purse

ONLY skilled smiths made sword blades patterned with steel, or inlaid axes. The smith cut the design into the blade in grooves and then hammered in silver wire.

leather sheath for dagger

LEATHER WORKERS made shoes, harnesses and saddlery.

ONLY RICH VIKINGS could afford clothes and armor as fine as the two jarls (above) are wearing. Poor men went into battle with a padded leather jerkin for protection instead of chain-mail. The man on the left has been to foreign places. His baggy trousers and fur hat are copied from styles worn by the Slavs who lived along the Russian rivers.

CARVING games helped pass winter evenings.

battle-ax

ARMOR and weapons were made by an armorer.

WOMEN wore a loose dress of wool or linen, and a shorter over-dress held by two big brooches. It often had a band of decoration at the hem. A shawl, pinned at the throat, was added for warmth.

scarf

brooch

shawl

Facts about Viking Dress:

For a Viking, lots of gold rings and armbands was today's equivalent of money in the bank. Goods could be paid for with jewelry or coins.

Women carried things they needed often – keys, knife, comb, scissors – on chains hanging from a brooch.

Married women covered their hair with a scarf.

Rubbing shoes with seal blubber waterproofed them.

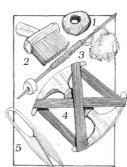

CLOTHMAKING tools: 1 Loom weight. 2 Comb for carding wool. 3 Spindle for spinning thread. 4 Reel for winding thread. 5 Shears.

WEAVING: weights kept the vertical warp threads taut. The weft threads were woven across them.

IMPORTED luxury goods: furs, silk, metalwork, glass and pottery.

FACT: VIKINGS WERE FINE SAILORS

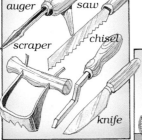

TRADING boats took goods along the coast.

USING a boat was part of a Viking's daily life. It was hard to get about overland, across mountains or through forests or bogs and, at times, deep snow. The simplest way, for all but the shortest journeys, was to use the rivers and coasts. Most Viking towns were on a river or coastal inlet, and nearby, at the water's edge, there was sure to be a shipyard – an open slope where boats were built and launched.

The Vikings were the most skilful boatbuilders and sailors of the north. They had boats for all purposes, from small river boats to ocean-going cargo ships, but they were most famed and feared for their warships: long, thin, square-sailed boats, crewed by up to 60 warrior-oarsmen. These ships were built to ride the stormy seas over which the Vikings sailed.

hammer
adze   ax   mallet
tongs
auger   saw
scraper   chisel
knife

SHIPBUILDERS' tools.

1 KNORR, sea-going cargo boat.
2 Coastal fishing boat. 3 Warship.

Facts about Viking Ships:

Vikings made the shell of a boat first, building it up from the keel with overlapping planks and then adding crosspieces. (Many boats are built the opposite way: inner framework first and then the sides.)

Vikings had no compasses. When out of sight of land, sailors judged where they were from the position of the sun or the stars.

crosspiece

ribs

rudder   hole for mast   oarhole

CARTS were used for short trips. Some cart bodies could be lifted from the wheel-base and loaded onto boats.

FINISHING a long ship (below). Viking ships had a single mast and were steered by a large rudder fixed to the starboard (right) side of the stern. Each oars-man sat on a chest containing his possessions.

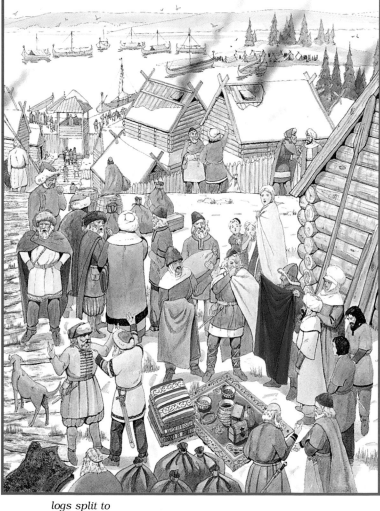

VIKING TRADERS sailed around the Baltic, getting stocks of costly northern goods: furs, amber and slaves seized in the Slav lands east of the Baltic. Vikings set up trading bases in these lands, like Staraja Ladoga (left) in northern Russia. It was at the end of a route from the south, along which Arab traders brought silks and spices to exchange for slaves and furs. Some Vikings took their boats south, via the Russian rivers, to the Black and Caspian Seas, where their goods sold for higher prices.

logs split to make planks

planks trimmed with adze

keel

VIKINGS did not fear the open sea and sailed far to find new lands. The house (right) made of stone and sods, as wood was scarce, was built by Vikings who reached Iceland.

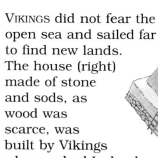

THE SECRET of the Vikings' success was surprise.
Their shallow ships carried them right onto the
beach. The raiders were rushing ashore before
their victims even realized they were coming.
They could attack inland towns, too, because
their longships could sail far upriver.

FACT: TO GO 'A–VIKING' MEANT TO GO RAIDING

FOR a Viking warrior raiding was a way of winning glory
and riches. Vikings were skilled sailors and fearless
fighters. When they realized that Christian lands to the
south were rich with treasures, the boldest could not
resist the temptation to go 'a-Viking'. Each raider swore to be
loyal to the rest and to share the plunder.

The Vikings first spread terror among Christians by an
attack in 793 on the monastery on the island of Lindisfarne, off
the north-east coast of England. They soon reappeared, making
lightning swoops in Britain, Germany, France, Spain and Italy.
Europe lived in fear of them for three centuries.

Viking coins

weapons at
the ready

longships
beached in
shallows

alarm-raisers
killed

MONASTERIES
were easy
targets, with
rich pickings.

Facts about Raiding:

Essentials for raiders: chain-mail
tunic, sword, spear, shield, broad-
ax and helmet.

Some rulers paid the Vikings to go
away. This protection money was
called Danegeld.

In the 9th century the raids became
invasions. Troops of Vikings would
make a base in a country, seize the
land and settle there permanently.

PEOPLE who
resisted the
raiders were
killed. Others
were taken
captive.
Important people
were held for
ransom. The rest
were sold as
slaves or thralls.

SWORD HILTS were
richly decorated.
A particularly fine
sword would be
treasured and
given a name.

FACT: MOST VIKINGS WERE FARMERS

WOMEN milked the cows, sheep and goats and made butter and cheese.

MOST Vikings were farmers. Those living near the sea went fishing too, and did some raiding, but most of their living came from the land. How they farmed depended on where they lived. In southern Sweden and Denmark there was plenty of level fertile land, good for crops and grazing animals. But farmers had less choice the further north they lived. The winters were colder and darker and most of the land was rocky. The only crop that grew well was grass, so the people depended on cattle and sheep.

When a farmer died his eldest son inherited the farm. Younger brothers got a share of the rest of their father's wealth, but if they wanted to farm they had to find land. They could buy it, or clear forest to get it, but eventually there was no more land suitable for farming. Sheep- and cattle-farmers need lots of land for pasture for their animals, so when there was no more land they faced a crisis. This is what drove many Vikings to sail and raid overseas.

EVEN on the poorest soils a family grew some oats or rye to give them flour for bread.

smithy

fish drying

CHILDREN helped to care for the farmyard poultry and the pigs.

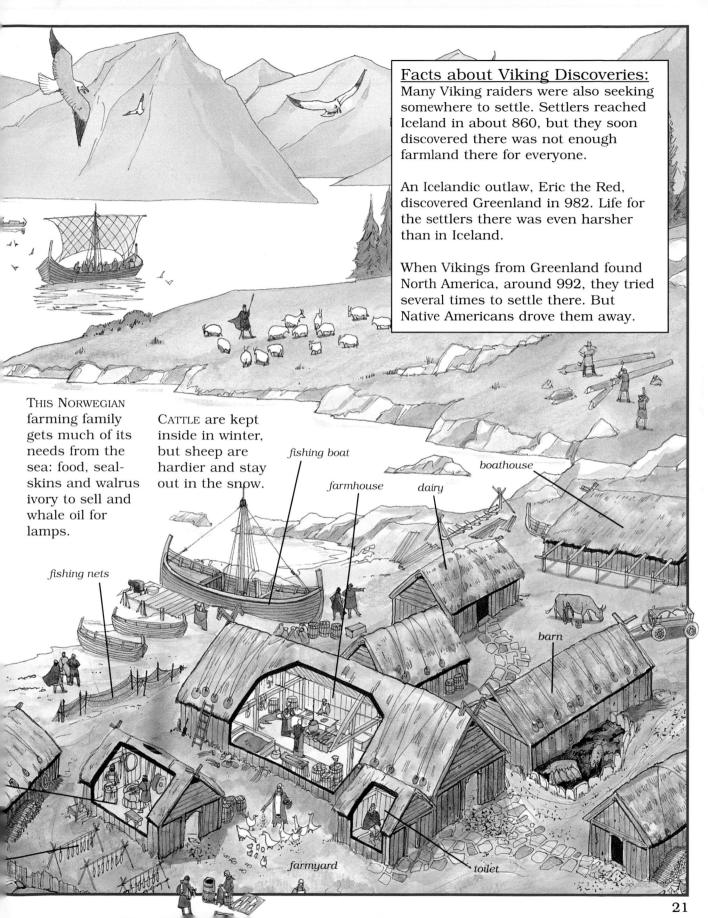

Facts about Viking Discoveries:
Many Viking raiders were also seeking somewhere to settle. Settlers reached Iceland in about 860, but they soon discovered there was not enough farmland there for everyone.

An Icelandic outlaw, Eric the Red, discovered Greenland in 982. Life for the settlers there was even harsher than in Iceland.

When Vikings from Greenland found North America, around 992, they tried several times to settle there. But Native Americans drove them away.

THIS NORWEGIAN farming family gets much of its needs from the sea: food, seal-skins and walrus ivory to sell and whale oil for lamps.

CATTLE are kept inside in winter, but sheep are hardier and stay out in the snow.

fishing boat

boathouse

farmhouse

dairy

fishing nets

barn

farmyard

toilet

21

FACT: VIKINGS WERE LAW-ABIDING CITIZENS

TWO sorts of law governed the way Vikings behaved. The first formed the basis of the Vikings' code of honor: they justified revenge, even if it involved what we would call arson or manslaughter. There were also laws stating the rules for inheriting property and describing various crimes and their punishments. Anyone who killed a man accidentally paid his relatives what he was worth, which depended on his status. The worst crimes were punished by banishment. Blood feuds could be ended by a grim type of accounting – one death cancelled out another of equal value.

A group of powerful local men acted as judges at an assembly of local freemen which was called the Thing. The laws were not written down. 'Lawmen' knew them by heart and taught the next generation.

LOCAL THINGS debated the affairs of a district, but important matters were settled at large regional ones. A Thing could last for several days. People who lived a good distance away brought their families and camped at the meeting place.

ATTENDING the Thing was a good way to meet old friends.

THINGS were held at set times each year, but in a crisis a special one could be called.

THINGVELLIR (Thing Valley), site of the Vikings' Althing.

FROM about 920 Icelanders held an assembly for the entire country – the Althing. It decided matters affecting the whole nation, so it was the first parliament.

APART from its serious business, the Althing was also a chance for a get-together, with sporting contests like wrestling, bareback racing and fights between champion stallions. It was also the place to trade and arrange a marriage. The Althing lasted two weeks and was the highlight of the year for many people.

Facts about Viking Laws:

At a trial, you needed relations to back you up. The judges might be influenced by a show of force.

Men struck their shields or rattled their spears to show their approval of a proposal at the Thing.

Women could not vote at the Thing and could only inherit their parents' property if they had no brothers.

THE LONGSHIPS of great jarls and the boats of small farmers line the water-front as people arrive for the open-air meeting of the Thing.

FACT: SOME CHRISTIAN SAINTS WERE VIKINGS

A LUCKY CHARM in the shape of Thor's hammer. Vikings believed this would protect them from harm.

IN SCANDINAVIA the Vikings worshiped gods like those that Germanic peoples had been worshiping for centuries: Odin, king of the gods and his wife Frigg, fiery-tempered Thor, treacherous Loki and many others. Religious ceremonies were held in temples or out of doors at a holy place, perhaps a grove of trees or a rock.

By the 9th century Vikings knew about Christianity from the Franks, the English and the Irish. Merchants who had been abroad spoke of it and raiders said the churches were packed with treasures. The first missionary arrived in Hedeby in 827, but the Vikings were not keen to become Christians when they learned they had to give up their old gods if they wanted to benefit from the new one. Thor was especially popular because he protected ordinary people who felt it would be unwise to desert him, though some people worshiped both. Later missionaries had more success. But some converts to Christianity had a practical motive. Converts were given new clothes on baptism, to symbolize their new life, so some Vikings turned up more than once.

THIS little figure is probably a Valkyrie. They were female spirits who took dead warriors to Odin's realm, greeting them with horns of ale.

DIFFERENT faiths met along the trade routes. Vikings met Muslim Arabs and Christian Franks. Christians preferred to trade with Christians, which probably encouraged Viking merchants to convert.

A PAGAN VIKING (right) buys from Muslim traders. Behind, another merchant bargains with a Frank.

AN ARAB traveler described how a Viking merchant in Russia prayed to his gods. He bowed before strange-looking figures and begged them to send him good luck in his trading.

HAVING it both ways: this pendant from Iceland was Thor's hammer hung one way, or a cross if hung the other. Icelanders almost had a civil war over whether to be Christian.

SMALL MODEL of the god Frey (above right). The Vikings believed he made crops grow, cattle thrive and couples have children.

A SMALL SILVER pendant of Christ crucified found in the grave of a Swedish Viking.

Facts about Viking Religion:

The Christian teaching Vikings found hardest to accept was the command to love one's enemies. Vikings did not believe in forgiveness.

The earliest Viking saint was Vladimir, ruler of the 'Rus' (Viking settlers in Russia) of Kiev. In 988 he made them all Christian. St Olaf, king of Norway, had been a great raider before he converted, He died in 1030, fighting pagan rebels.

SOME Vikings sacrificed humans to their gods, but most used animals. At Hedeby they were put on scaffolds outside houses.

VIKINGS learned of Christianity from Christians sold as thralls (above).

Vikings who settled in France, England or Ireland soon adopted the religion of their new land. By the 11th century pagan Vikings in Norway, Sweden and Denmark were also Christian. Their rulers had decided for religious and political reasons that it was better to be Christian, so everyone had to convert.

FACT: A GOOD DAY'S FIGHTING ENDED IN A FEAST

A SKALD did not exactly sing his poems. He half-sang half-chanted them, as he played a harp. Through these poems events were recorded and became legends without being written down.

A YOUNG man wanting adventure might spend several years in the service of a king or chief, before settling down to farm or trade. A great chief kept a band of armed men who were fiercely loyal to him. He fed and housed them and in return they fought for him whenever he wanted. At the end of their service he rewarded them well – with gold rings and armbands, fine weapons and rich clothes – after all, they had been prepared to die for him. A chief was expected to be generous. It proved he could obtain all the wealth he wanted – by raiding if necessary.

All Vikings, rich or poor, were as hospitable as they could afford to be. A chief entertained his men to lavish feasting and ale-drinking in his great hall. A king or very powerful jarl kept a special retainer, a skald, who sang while the warriors feasted. It was the skald's duty to make poems praising the brave deeds of his chief.

ON A DARK winter evening everyone enjoyed listening to a story. Tales of the gods were popular. There were many good stories about Thor, the storm god, whose hammer-blows made the thunder. One tells how Thor lost his hammer. It was stolen by the giant Thrym, who would only give it up if he could have the goddess Freya as his wife. Thor dressed up in women's clothes and pretended to be Freya. He fooled the giant and killed him, and so got his hammer back. The tales of Odin were more mysterious and frightening. It was said that in order to learn wisdom he hanged himself for nine days and nights upon the magic ash tree, Yggdrasil. Through this ordeal he became master of all knowledge, including a powerful secret that, in great pain, he tore from the darkness – the secret of the runes, the symbols that make up the Vikings' alphabet.

Facts about Feasting, Fighting and Legends:

Warriors looked forward to endless battles and feasts after their death. In Valhalla, Odin's Hall of the Slain, they would fight and kill each other by day and then become whole again and feast together as friends.

Pagan Vikings did not write down their history or beliefs. All we know about them comes from clues found by archaeologists, and from the sagas and records of people who met them, such as their Christian neighbors (and victims) and the Arabs.

In 13th-century Iceland scholars wrote down the stories of their ancestors. These written versions are the sagas.

FEASTING and drinking were favorite Viking pastimes. Special feasts could last several days. There were feasts to mark seasonal festivals like mid-winter Yule (replaced by Christmas), as well as feasts for weddings and funerals.

RUNES recording brave deeds were cut on large standing stones.

THE Vikings' runes were made up of 16 different symbols.

VIKINGS had no paper. They cut runes into wood or stone.

FEW VIKINGS could read or write, so understanding runes gave power.

As a result the Vikings believed the runes were magical.

THEY also thought the runes could be used to cast spells.

FACT: A GLORIOUS DEATH WAS BETTER THAN A LONG LIFE

LIFE for most Vikings was a struggle for survival against bad weather, poor soil, attacks from neighbors, unexpected accidents and untreatable illnesses. Viking medical knowledge was limited to a few herbal remedies and a trust in magic spells and charms. So it is not surprising that the average life expectancy was only 50 years, but this did not worry many Vikings. In their tough lives there was no advantage in lingering on with stiffening joints and increasing pain.

A Viking warrior hoped to meet his end in battle. Such a glorious death would be praised in song when the fighting was over and the feasting began. It would win him a place in Valhalla and his name would be remembered whenever people spoke of fearless deeds.

The sagas also describe the deeds of brave women, but most women had to spend their lives looking after their home and family. They only ran the family farm or business if their husband was away raiding or on a long journey.

FOR a woman, childbirth was a dangerous time. (It was for the baby too.) Her life was hard, and unless she was a strong character she had few choices in it.

EVEN if they were not full-time warriors, men usually met a violent death.

A 'STRAW DEATH' (dying at home on your mattress) was despised.

VIKINGS believed in being clean. Some homes had outdoor lavatories and some people enjoyed saunas.

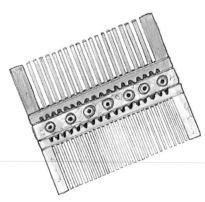

ABOVE: WALRUS ivory scoop (left) used to clean the ears. Double-sided combs (right) could be used for hair and beards.

TWO MEN enjoying a sauna (below).

VIKINGS believed in an afterlife. Kings and jarls were given fine funerals to speed them to the next world.

FUNERAL customs varied from place to place. Some pagan Viking peoples buried their dead, others cremated them. In both cases it was usual to surround the corpse with objects that the dead person would need in the afterlife, such as food, weapons and tools. Horses and dogs (and sometimes slaves) were killed to accompany their master or mistress.

Facts about Viking Burials:

Two burial ships over 70 feet long have been found in Norway.

The Oseberg ship, built about 800, held a woman, her female servant, a wagon, cooking equipment and personal objects. The Gokstad ship, of about 850, held a man, 12 horses, 6 dogs and 3 rowing-boats.

MANY things suggest the Vikings believed death was a voyage to another land. Graves were often outlined by stones in the shape of a boat. Sometimes real boats were used as coffins. A great chief would be buried in an entire longship.

VIKINGS who cremated their dead honored a great chief with a ship-burning. An Arab merchant wrote about one he saw on the River Volga in Russia in 922. The dead chief was embalmed and dressed in silk clothes. His ship was brought ashore, propped up on stakes and firewood was piled underneath. Then a tent was put up on the deck. The chief was put inside, together with a live slave-girl. Then the ship was set on fire.

CHRISTIANITY put an end to such customs. Christians had to be buried in holy ground.

GLOSSARY

Adze Tool with the blade at right angles to the handle, for shaping wood.

Arson Crime of deliberately setting fire to property.

Auger Tool used to bore holes.

Carding Combing raw wool to straighten the fibers before spinning it into thread.

Daub Mixture of mud and straw.

Dowry Goods or money given to a couple on marriage by the parents of the bride.

Frankish Belonging to the empire of the Franks, who lived in what is now France and Germany.

Freeman Man or woman who was not a slave.

House-burning Deliberately setting fire to a house (and those inside), as a revenge.

Keel Long wooden beam forming the bottom of a boat.

Quern Device for grinding grain into flour, made of two stones. The top one, turned by a handle, crushed the grain against the bottom one.

Rampart A protective mound of earth topped by a wall.

Runes The symbols of the Vikings' alphabet.

Sagas Traditional stories of Viking heroes, first written down in the 13th century.

Soapstone Type of stone that is easy to carve. It is common in parts of Scandinavia,

Sods Blocks of cut turf.

Thing-stead Site where meetings of a Thing were held.

Warp Threads which run lengthways in woven material.

Wattle Woven paneling made of stakes and flexible twigs.

Weft Threads woven across fabric through the warp threads.

INDEX